I0547216

DEEP DIVE POETRY

DEEP DIVE POETRY

Maria Sonia Orsini

2024

Universalist Poetry/North Carolina, USA

DEDICATION

To my father and my mother. I love you with all my heart!

CONTENTS

DEEP DIVE POETRY

Silent Waves

To Kuldeep

You came like a silent wave to our lives.
We did not know you.
We only knew that you were our silent wave.
Silent waves only exist on those who do not know
you.
And how that rapidly change!

Having you in our team of dolphins.
Having you jump and laugh to the rhythm of the
waves surrounding us.
But mostly the silent wave within you.
What a silent and dark sea to be when you can't
share your thoughts.

3

What a scary place to be when you do not know
when the tallest wave is coming to smash you.
Laughing dolphins around you, made you laugh.
Dancing dolphins around you made you want to
dance.
The silent wave that it was, was no more.
We could hear your soul and empty our empty hearts
with your kindness and love.
We could hear loud and clear your silent wave
coming from far away, getting closer and closer to us.
So close, that the rampant sound has made a clear
difference in our lives.
We are happier than before because of you!
Silent wave you are no more.

Cancer

Talking about cancer.
Comfort zone, none!

I was young, scared, and overwhelmed.
I ran in fear.
Raced to hiding.
Too much to bear at close sighting.

Years passed by when I
Saw you, cancer again.
Moving slowly but surely
you sneaked home, no gain.

Not in me. Again.
Not trying to brag.

Lucky me, so sad.

My home sign says, "Cancer is not welcome",
But don't cross that door.
Come see this.
Cancer came back rushing, hunting.
Punched us hard in the gut, neck, and back.
And back we fought back,
just as hard. Very hard!

Not once, not twice, but many times.
Like an eighteen-wheeler crashed smashed!
We screamed:
"Just leave now!

But the triggering trigger stop, nope.
So, we won't stop hope.
Cancer may spell hopelessness.
Not for us, never for us.

And the fate wrongly spoken,
By those who are supposed to know, wonder.
No more wasted tears.
Cancer may spell giving up.
Not for us, never for us.

Relentless, faith gave us hope.
And when the pain, puking, and tiredness seem to be
all,
we knocked hard at God's front door.

Pleading like rhythmic stars.
Tired, yes tired.
Begging for it to stop.
Kneeling, yes kneeling,
Enough is enough.

Not wanting to hear about it.
Not wanting to talk about it.
None of it Anymore.
I heard a knocking,
Two and three.

Railroad Crossing

Life is a railroad crossing.
Ready I was to keep on going.
My pedal pressed hard to the floor,
Did not last long.
Brake! I braked.
Suddenly braked.
Suddenly, no more tomorrow.

Life is a railroad crossing.
Didn't see it coming.
And what excuses would I have for those waiting?

9

Who would take the time to wait?
Who would believe me?

Life is a railroad crossing.
I see short and long cabooses pass by me.
Short ventures full of exiting adventures.
And survived to tell it!
And long ventures that are boring
Only worth remembering.

Life is a railroad crossing.
Fast, so fast, I cannot recognize faces past the whirly
winds.
Low, so slow, that I can't wait to end the wait.

Time to move on.
Don't' worry.
Longing will come again with the next stop,
At the railroad crossing.

Faces of Faith

Faces of Faith I have seen,
Through me and you.
All unique.
Like a pearl.
Take my faith as a pearl ring.
Wear it every day.
Because it is not like any other ring.

Faces of Faith
I saw in an old woman.
35 years later,
After sickness and dreadful news, she survived.
She confronted those with laugh.
Laughed when awakened.
Laugh before bed.
Laugh, laugh, and more laugh!

"Free to use", she said,
Laugh was her Face of Faith.

Another Faith of Faith.
This time for the agnostic.
That one!
The one who turned his head away,
Every time not certain.
Who cares? as I faithful was there.
And His Name I called,
Sincere faith bestowed.
The miracle was done,
And the agnostic was no more.

And when the Face of Faith
Is needed.
When everything else looks foggy.
Hope foggy.
Future foggy.
Slow - down, faith says.
Minute to minute counts.
Minutes to live.
Minutes is all I really have.

Hours- too long.
And days too far in the horizon
For the orange morning skies to be seen
And a future to hold.

And in the Face of Who knows,
A stronger Face of Faith shows up.
The Faith of Face that cannot go,
even in the Face of Loss.

It does not take pandemics,
Speed of light, or torrents of water to have faith.
The Face of Faith is like a microscopic
Drop of water.
Life can live in water,
No matter how small.
Fruitful trees can bear fruit where a dry slate was
carved,
And a drop, drop, was dropped.
And when the thirst has dropped you to your knees,
that small drop can quench your thirst.

And one drop of water can change your life.
For if we do not seek minute to minute
To find that drop.
Drink from my glass.
Count on me,
With love.

Friend Death

Death is my destiny.
Loud and clear.
Death is my friend.
Not my enemy.

But making death worth a thought is my struggle.
And while some may feel
Pains and battles
Are their sorrows.
With hope and faith, I claim,
pain make me victorious.

And when death feels alive
Fame and money are worthless,
And a million hearts and thumbs useless.
Friend death gets me.

15

As with every sundown whispers
Tears of hope, faith, and wisdom.

And inspiration worth a trillion starts I found,
Writing poems to my friend death,
Who is delighted hearing me deaf.
Deaf to artificial tongues.
Deaf to artificial tones.
Deaf to artificial people.

My friend death recalls,
There is no time to waste,
With soul killers hunting your dreams at best.
Chaining our minds
And starving our hopes.
Because inspired those are
to seek our death before we are done.

"Do not succumb earlier than death,
 to artificial cries and touts",
my friend death said.
Jump high, dance crazy, and hit your drum hard,
Be you Loud.
Be you Harder.
Be you Louder.
Drum, drum, drum,
All the way until your friend death calls.
Or until your neighbor calls the cops.

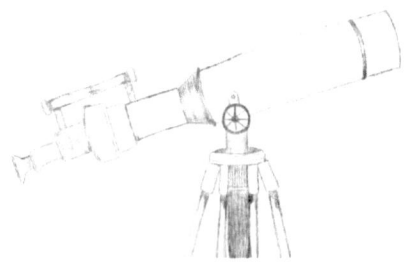

For the Leader in You

For the Leader in you, I could build a house.
But it won't be big enough to hold your caring smile,
or to hold all the people who you have impacted.

Fort the leader in you, I could build a supersonic jet,
But it won't be fast enough to reach the star in which
you were standing,
looking at the big picture, from far away.

For the leader in you, I could send you to wild forests
to find the most beautiful and exotic birds in Earth.
But it won't be enough because you have already
found the wild key for innovation.

For the leader in you, I could dress in white to show
you how much I love nursing.
But it won't be enough because you have a closet full
of hats,
and you love to wear ALL of them.

17

For the leader in you, I could get you a trans galactic telescope.
But it won't be enough because your vision goes beyond the speed of light.

For the leader in you, I seek to be one like you in the future.
But it won't be enough, because for the leader in you, every second counts now,
for what you are present now.

For the leader in you, I am grateful to know you.
But it won't be enough because I can see you in all your mentees,
And all the people that you have coached and helped grow through the years.

For the leader in you, this is my poem to you.

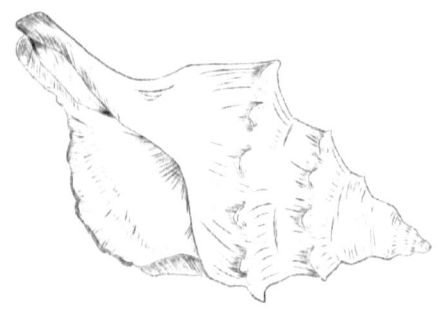

Passing By

Life is something.
Something to be delighted to.
And we never know what is next.
But we know what is now.
Life is like finding unique shells in the sand.

I picked up a shell this light morning,
and there it was, all alone.
It was empty,
a beautiful skeleton, perhaps a star fish,
But empty.

I picked up another shell this evening.
The sky was bright orange.
Coarse in the outside and slick in the inside.
Looked inside, beautiful greens, blues, and yellows.
Never knew.
All in one.

19

And shining through.
Melting our joy with the sand.

And the next shell I picked was at night.
The core was light and heavy.
And the lining was hard and tender.
My heart rejoiced.

This last one, I passed once,
and nothing is the same.
Laughs sometimes, tears another.
Never dullness.
Navigating together through the hard winds,
And elevating the sails
every time I needed to stern.
Steady and gracefully passed me bye.
Return to your vast ocean,
Where every place is home.

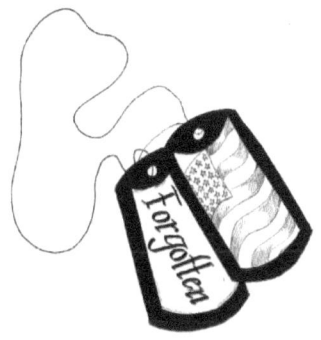

The Forgotten

Flying through your memory of Vietnam
A past gone behind, but never left.
A blinding flash, still flashing, of how your pain was
forgotten.

Tears dropped quickly and a silent pause, long
becomes before me.
A knot in my throat and then my tears knocked.
Together in a moment.
We.
Silent.

A memory that did not belong to me,
but you wanted to.
More than anything else.

A longing, long longing,
that your service would be remembered, by all!
And that your service

would not be stifled by the medals earned by others
in far lands.

Yours were unique, just like your scars.
I could see it in the wetness of your eyes.
You knew that I wasn't there before,
to wipe your tears.
But I am here now.
Brother, Sister, come in here.

As the Nurse Enters the Veteran's Room

As you enter the Veteran's room,
The unexpected happens.
You speak with the Veteran fast, walk fast, and call
for help fast.
Because you care fast.
With your boss you speak,
And with your staff you debrief.
So much stress, but you are so resilient.
Not much time to speak your truth to the universe,
Because the next Veteran is waiting.

As you enter the Veteran's room,
Routine you expected,
But the unexpected happens.
Veteran's family gathers around you,
And said, "Thank you for doing your best".
Plus, they brought chocolate covered jingle bells,
that song songs of hope, peace, and health.

And the best gift of all, the Veteran's words:
"And as you gave me another chance,
I will see you again.
And I will sing a song or two dedicated just for you,
Happy to say this again, soon with love, I love you."

Only Took Once

It only took once,
To see your suffering.
War images that traveled away
in dusty dry smelly funky air.

It took me only once,
To stop saying I won't look at you, suffering,
Because I knew that looking would make me move.

It took me only once,
Seeing children dying,
What else could I do, but crying?

It took me only once,
To image how much loneliness, anxiety, thirst, and
hunger

those images of children gifted to my spoiled life.

It took me only once,
To feel how my daily vanity,
vanished quickly.
And in the middle of despair and hopelessness of
millions of children,
I couldn't do anything, but just cry.
Once. Just once.

 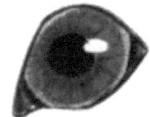

Your Eyes

Your black eyes
Starred at me
with glittering sunlight love
in your darkest night.

I recall your eyes,
Forever powerful.
And there is nothing,
I rather do.
Your eyes filled me with a sea of love,
caring, kindness,
Like soft tender clouds.
Really like?
Not really, nothing to compare to.

I.
"Don't stop staring at me.
Please, don't go!

Do not leave me!"

Please, stay longer and don't blink.
I want to engrave your staring love forever in my
dreams.
Time to go.
Time to sleep.
See you tonight black eyes.
Forever in my dreams.

Broken Heart

What can mend my broken heart?
Nothing.
Memories don't work,
And a million tears I have shed.

Trying to relive when you followed me,
When you sat with me,
When you played with me,
And the most special of it all,
When you danced with me.

With every memory
My chest grows tighter.
And my contained tears,
They also, try to be a fighter.
It doesn't work.

29

I had to let those go,
But I can't let you go.
No pain like this jut stops.

Wish I could see you again,
Hear you again.
Dance with you again.
But only ashes I have left,
And no place to pour them away.
There is none. And nada can mend my broken heart.

I Finally Get it Mama

Mama mia. My mother.
You sang me lullabies so many times.
"Again", I said,
Repeating the songs
Tiredly, it seems.
But it was not, you just loved me so much.

Tired she was so tired.
Cooking,
Washing dishes,
And washing clothing by hand.
So many chores. Tire she was.

But most tiring
And I did not understand then,
It was my brother.
My brother with a mental disability
That put my mother to her limits.
Tired she was.

31

Couldn't understand then,
But I can now.
Myself, mentally tired.

Teaching my kid,
Who takes many teachers.
He is loving and thoughtful,
And prays for the strangers.

But sometimes, a handful
can't describe how difficult it becomes.
Like being in a tornado
That suddenly is born.

Patience and for more patience
I pray for.
Because the Lord knows how much, is much enough.

And the peace, without knock,
Suddenly comes.
But my brain waves
Are still pulsating with nuclear force.

Mama mia.
I finally understand.
Please, forgive me.
It took me so long.
And now I love you more.

The Jailer

Inside you is a prison
That you are not aware of.
Confidence left you early on
And in the dust of the hourly hand
Your timer seems to be running back door.

Your willingness
To let me risk small moments,
Small craziness that invites joy,
Are gone.
Dullness grows.

Breathing with a jailer is suffocating.
But a healthy living reminder
of not giving up.

The jailer does not feel in control,
So, taking your control
Wins them up.

33

A jailer forgets you need to live,
and forgets you are alive.
But I know I am.
I do not forget to live, I am alive.

Fearless I am,
and strong I feel,
because I am free.

Reconvening all
prisoners of the jailer,
One stands out.
The freedom that came without fear.
Martin Luther King Jr. fought in peace,
And did not keep silent.
Disrupter he was.
Disrupting,
marched, marched, marched.

And I also have a dream.
To lose the jailer's keys.
The key to fear.
The key to ashamedness.
The key to procrastination.
The key to untrust.
The key to lethargy.
The key to habit.
The key of the ordinary.
And the key to mediocracy.

Breaking out
through the walk of melting shames,
And the fire of the names.
Freedom!
Run!
Freedom!
Run fast,
Run, be free!

For the Love of Nature

For the love of nature,
I hear songs of greens, blues, and yellows.
I love your waters, moons, and meadows.

Nature speaks to me.
Harmony, peace, and strength, endless love,
I love You nature.

Your fingertips warm my waters of the tropics and
Fill me with bioluminescent shine.
Like a sky full of trillions of tiny little stars
Calling me high and low
to love you more, nature.

Greens fill my heart with wonder and mysteries of
nature.
Irreplaceable feeling

37

When running wild through your rivers and
mountains.
Oh, green, I love you.

And when my friend called me,
We could not stop talking gratitude for the daily
travels we made.
Surrounded by trees, right and left,
Full of trees. So much love we felt, nature.

I opened the window and breathed deep.
Deep as the caverns.
Pure air, I felt you.
Oh, I love you.

Greens and browns together
Like a dance between grand sequoias standing tall.
As tall as the sky
I wish to touch.
What a beautiful sight.
Closer to heaven I feel,
When standing close to you, nature.

Garden Flowers

Emotional tears of happiness
Rolled down my chin,
Like a flash flood warning.

A beautiful ceramic vase
Mixed tones of green, blue, and gray
Resembling dark heavenly rain.

The vase is full of majestic flowers.
Collected by you,
From the garden.

Mixed like a rainbow,
Knock out pink roses,
Red thorny roses,
And large purple and white irises.

39

How much nurturing love
Nature gives to us.
And how much love you give me.

Unearthing the meaning of love,
Is not like unearthing a
million-dollar treasure hunt.

Unearthing love hugs you tight to
The plain smell of dirt in your hands
From your loving heart.
You handed me flowers from our garden.
Love I felt, my love.

Author Bio

Maria Orsini, EdD, MSN, RN finds inspiration in daily experiences that may bring you dive down emotions of hurt, hope, faith, love, and beauty. Because Maria has been a registered nurse for 30 years, some of her poems show the high sense of advocacy that she has for patients and their families. She hopes that you are inspired to be your true self and write your own story. Maria holds a doctorate's degree in educational leadership from University of Phoenix, Arizona, and has lived in Butner, North Carolina, since 1996. Contact Maria at dr.maria.orsini@gmail.com to request permission for reproduction. All rights reserved.

Illustrator Bio

Haley Bannister is a commission-based illustrator and artist based in Virginia. She specializes in digital illustration and watercolor painting, favoring realism and portraiture. She is inspired by emotion and the natural beauty of life, and loves to paint plants, animals, landscapes, and people. Haley is finishing her degree in English Literature from the University of St. Andrews, where she developed a love of figure drawing as an active member of their Art Society. Haley is excited for this to be her first contribution to a published work and hopes that her illustrations help the reader connect in a more meaningful way to the powerful poetry of Dr. Orsini.

41